BIRCH

Poems of Love

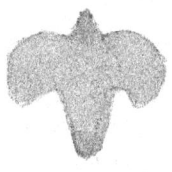

Elizabeth Anne Hin

Copyright © 2018 Elizabeth Anne Hin
All Rights Reserved

Illustrations Copyright © 2018 by Cynthia L. Kirkwood

Editing, Design, & Composition by Sarla V. J. Matsumura

Library of Congress Control Number: 2018946509

ISBN-13: 978-0692106662
ISBN-10: 0692106669

Printed in the United States of America

Published by Issa Press
Austin, Texas

DEDICATION

To John David Gabriel
Kirsten Elise Gabriel
John Taylor Gabriel
Mackenzie Meredith Gabriel

CONTENTS

Three	1
Wren Song	5
Jdg	9
I Took Her Hand	11
Baby Wrens	21
Darling	23
Our Cardinal	25
Once	27
Graduating	29
The Vow	31
Always	43
Son	47
Roses	51
She	53
Voice	57
His Love	75
The Love of My Life	77
Sanctuary	79

THREE

Petals of
The
Sacred
Awaken
In
My
Heart
Three
Children

Three

Of
My soul

Several thousand I am with
In prayer

And all life

But
Three
Rise

Roses
In bud

Toward
Heaven
God remembered
And not

My God~Mothering
Step~Mothering
Toward
Their

Faith
Hope

And all
Breath

Toward
Heaven

In
All
Of the
Names
And ways

Of our
Love

Toward
That
One

Is not
That
My place

As
Mother

Their
Rose stems
Reaching
Toward
Earth

To
Know
And
Be

Each
To
Become
Enbloomed
In life
A
Great
Soul
A
True
Soul
Humble
Real
Always
In
Dignity
And
Grace

My
Son
And
Two Daughters
Piaf, elder
And
Little one

Roses

Blooming
Three
This
Mother's Day
And
Always

My
Bouquet

Every
Day

Is
Mother's Day
For me
For this woman
For this daughter

Three children

My
Roses
Of
Heaven

Roses
Bouquet
Of
Heaven

WREN SONG

If

I
Were
A
Wren
I would

Build
A
Nest
With
You

Flitting
With
Tuft
Of willow
Silk
In
My

Tiny
Strong
Beak

Tail
Alift
As I
Seek

Down
And
Twig
Strand
Of
Grass
Leaf
And
Branchlet

So eternity
Might
Be born

In our
Little
White
Home

Birdhouse

At our
Kitchen
Door

Oh
And
When
His
Song
Comes
Into
All
Around
Him
This
Spring

That
Wren
Father's
Song

Such joy.

JDG

John
I here everywhere know you and only you
You and you and only you
You, you, only you
Always
Anywhere
Everywhere
Ever
Where
Here

I TOOK HER HAND

I.

Almost old now, I look Heavenward from
 this Earth
Toward the azure blue of day, the deep
 starlight of night
Beyond all weather, season, blessing,
 gift of life, heartbreak of loss, of death
From before our Ancestors, through them,
 the honored spirit of their promise
 within us, and beyond us

I remember our Children, Grandchildren,
 their hoped~for Children to come,
And my marriage, a holy love, a great,
 true love
For there are some things I know

From before we were born
I took her hand.

II.
In youth, birth to boy, to young
  man
Raised that I might be, each and all days
  of my life
Strong, modest, dignified, regular, rare,
  real
My own self, ordinary ~ yet not

Nice shirt, hands work~honed or at the
  wheel of a truck
Sun~burnished face, sleeves rolled up,
  tending errands, chores, every day
That I might be fair, be and become truly
  good
With a slight gift of humor
Sometimes an ember of lit fire, too

I met her, a woman hard~described
  by me in words
Woman of Columbine, Poppy,
  Lupen and Paintbrush
Climbing creamy Jasmine, rambling dusty
  Rose
Yucca, Ocotillo
And pale tawny Almond Blossom
A woman as if a living flower, leaf, vine,
  root
Perfuming my soul, my
  heart, my life

This true bouquet of a woman
I took her hand.

III.
Man I am, good man I aspire to be
Before I kissed her
With my maturing palm, open
   fingers, sinewed arm, and supple wrist
Dedicated toward wisdom, prudence,
   patience, success, and grace
Nervous beside her without reins or
   steering wheel in hand
Leaned out, a mild bit, a slight turn
   toward her, like a light breeze
   might, and with about all that I am

And ever will be
I took her hand.

IV.
Groves of trees and fields ~ fertile and
   fair
Heavy and filled with harvest some years,
   some years spare and dry
My flower, my bouquet, in all seasons
   gloriously harvesting her love and living
   faith into seedlings as jams in
   jars, bundles of nuts into sacks
Her life blossomed to render us fulfilled in
   meaning and life, gifts of kitchen,
   hearth, flower petals of porch and quilt
Wisdom, fresh air, firelight, cool drink

Her strength steadfast, enduring, as
   Matriarch of our era
Heaven's gifts to us, lean year or
   bountiful
As we journey a bit to the hunt and tell
   tales of past proffered stags whose
   spirits bless us still
And will bless us always
She prepares grains, vegetables and pie,
   baking, preserving into the very day
   the center of our Family's story,
The safe knowledge that this good man,
   and every one of us

Is home, now, and always
I take her hand.

V.

At the New Year, in the ribbons of
   Christmas, birth of child, and after
In quietude, before all that was and is,
   toward all that might be
As morning dawns and nighttime dusks
Her soul's wings open and close as if the
   wings of a Monarch Butterfly or those
   of our other favorite types,
The yellow types, and the dun in mottled
   earthen hues
And the vibrant blue butterflies near our
   cabin

My winged flower butterfly woman
I take your hand.

VI.
Before the wedding, now six decades
 past
Sequoias standing sentinel, off in forests
 not so far East of us
Ocean breezes to our West, moisture
 struggling to us over the low Coastal
 range
Their echo of tide and wave within our
 hearts

I, content, might say so or not, converse
 or not, like wind and tree, like so much
 that we love

Teasing or serious, strong and
 resilient, attentive and vulnerable
I take her hand.

VII.
From out of eternity, at our wedding,
    before I turned at the altar
I didn't tell anyone ~ no need
Heaven and I were discussing, in silence
As we have always done, and like to do
Candles burning, flowers bedecked
Faint scent of incense and ceremony in my
    heart

That thus before the vows aloud and
    ascribed of books and priests, laws
    and history
I vowed in my own unshakeable promise
Silently, deep as our mountains, plains,
    and storms
As all lightning, thunder, and rainbow
As all waterfall, rainfall, and beauty of
    this good Earth, all
Sunlight and moonlight, all life, all creation
All that is, that ever was, that ever shall be

Before that altar, at that altar
I took her hand.

VIII.
I never told anyone what I said and did
In this soul of mine, this heart, this life
About my wife, for her, to her
At the altar of God
There is no conversation for love this deep
This wisdom of love is ours, hers and mine
Always
This is marriage.

In each loss and gain
As she stacks jars to nurture me
One fruit and another
Dried nuts, setting aside these, my favorite
Fussing over me, for me, and against me
From worn shirt to dirty boot and
Irritated husband needing her comfort

Old stallion that I am, unmanaged wild
Creature
Bear, eagle or, songbird
Tending me all the while, as if she were a
Mustang, a mountain lioness,
A songbird trilling, flying back to me at our
Nest
My wing mended, my broken paw
Soothed, my aging pride content
Our freedom exalts in goodness together,
Throughout all time

She is my Wife.
So beautiful to me.
Before God, this day
And always
I take her hand.

For Jacare Cardoza's Beloved
Maternal Grandparents,
James and Annette Maiorino

BABY WRENS

Today
Baby Wrens
Bless
This Spring day
And every day
In this
Song of God
I live
With you.

DARLING

Darling
Only one
Thought of
Called by
That name
Darling
Always
Everywhere
Only
One
Only
You

Darling

OUR CARDINAL

The wrens are here
The wrens are here
And you,
My Darling

Tiny nuthatches
Call in song
As fine and sweet
As the voices
Of Hummingbirds

In the morn
As you
Awaken
To work

All of
Mankind
Is healed
As you
Enter the day

Almost
Each day
Bluejays come
Unafraid
Unabashed

And enjoy
Our feeder
At branches
Of Pecan
Crepe Myrtle
Willow
And Mesquite

Later
Is the call
Of a Dove
And then,
Another

The Cardinal comes
And you speak in joy
You turn to me
And to him
And tell me
There he is

ONCE

Once
Upon a time
He believed in cowboys
Sweet songs
With fiddles
Sometimes mandolins
Men singing
Men and women
Striving in church
And heroes
With capes
Father and Grandfathers
And himself
Like them
She believes him,
Always has.

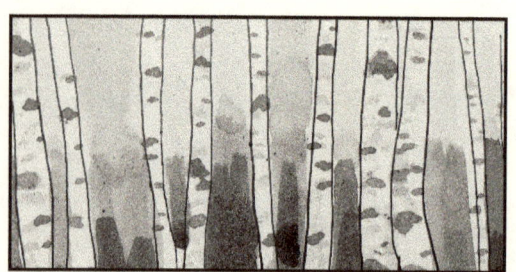

GRADUATING

Your Father regarded
His face turned
Before us
To a tree
Whose name
I do not know
High in a grove
Of Redwoods
Eldest perhaps
Five centuries
At the canopy
And just beneath
A hummingbird
Large, mature, strong, real,
And alive
Filled with the deep
Springtime morn
Sought nectar
Above us
At the canopy of the audience
Heads, hats, and a parasol
Flew a Dragonfly
Large, majestic, iridescent, real,
Flitting, hovering, diving, arising,
One Crow or Raven
Left to right
And
Right to left
Witness
Silent
With us all
As you
Graduating adorned
In waist~length hair
Dress of evening~sky lace

Garland of orchids bedecked
Robes of academic meaning
And excellence
And then you were blessed
By running stream
At the base
Of those
So beautiful
Creatures' home
Where you have dreamt, arisen,
Walked, contemplated, decided,
And acted
Noble, brilliant and true
Our Hummingbird Girl
Dragonfly Daughter
Eucalyptus Scholar
Redwood woman
We are blessed.

For Mackenzie Meredith Gabriel

THE VOW

On
The
Day

Of
The
Wedding

The
Whole
Earth

Breathed

A
Vow

In
Silent
Promise

Yes

Birds
Prayed
As
The
Very
Song
Of
Dawn

And
Every
Infinitesimal
Droplet

Of
Moisture
Arising

Into
The sky

To become
Clouds

To become
Someday

Rain
Into
Ocean

Every
Droplet
Answered

Yes

I
Do
We
Do

We
All
Do
All
That
Is
Water
Anywhere
Everywhere

Dolphins
Leapt

Spoke

To
Whales
Their
Great
Friends

Oh
Yes
I do
We do

Whales
Responded

Pilot whales
Great Blues

And
Tender
Greys

We all
Do

Deer
Of
Earth

Stag
Doe
Fawn

To
Elder
Roan
Axis
Red
Mule
Whitetail

Snorted
And
Whispered

All
Creatures
Roared
Chirped
Cooed
Howled
Bayed
Barked
Whispered
And
Called

Yes
All

As
Above
Them
The fire
That
Is
Sun

Who
Had
Always
Promised

Yes

To
God

Creator
Originator
Of
All
Of
This

Orchestration
Of
Universe

Burned
With

This
Complete
Ocean
Of
Droplets

This
Pure
Radiant
Fire

Sublime
Vast
Air

Wise
Beautiful
Earth

With

Beloved
Creatures
Of
Sentience
And
Grace

Into
Eternity

Into
Every
Discreet

Moment

Of
All
Time

Everywhere

Such
Love
Self~evident
And
True

Trees
Flowers
Grasses
All
That
Is
Plant
Expressed
A
Bouquet
A
Boutonnière
Of
Life
Of
Trunk
Stem
Leaf
Bud
Blossom
And
Seed

Above
All
Flowers
Branches
And
Roots

The
Luminous
Moon
Reflected
Of
Sun

That
The Man
And
The Woman

Appear

To
Have
Been
Wed

By
All
That
Is

Was

And
Ever
Shall be

In
Hymn

Of
Dolphin
Song

Whale
Voice

Deer
Flicker
And
Call

In
Blessing

Of
Garden
Bouquet
A
Garland

In
Sunlight
Moonlight
Starlight

On
This
Day
This
Night

Of
The
Wedding

And

Always.

For Jdg in his sixty~fifth year,
With gratitude to the poetry, life, and example of Czeslaw Milosz

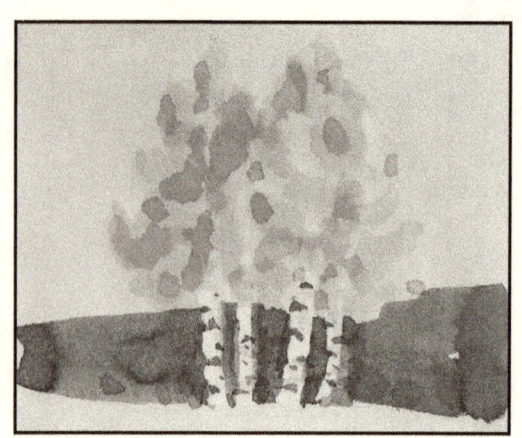

ALWAYS

One day
You will turn
Toward the sun
And
The moon

Your precious soul
Will say
Look Maman
And
Remember

That I am
Not here
Beside you
Beneath
The cloud reflected
The crescent
The golden rays
Starlight
Grace of Heaven
Upon this Earth

My body
Will have
Gone
To dust
As you regard
The Milky Way
Or newest book
Of ideas
You had not
Contemplated
Before the author
But do with her

Or him
Now
In brilliance
Innovation
And
Such
Fierce and tender
Love

But not
On
This day

One day
You will argue
With your companion
Or spouse
Your child
If blessed
To have one
Your sister
Or brother
And
Remember

That I am
Here
Beside you
In birdsong
Morning dew
Evening light
All grace

You will cease
Arguing
Tears arising
In your
Eternal
Doe eyes
Of grace
And
God

And
You will be
Maman's daughter
Embodying
Love
As do
The Saints
And
Sages
Noble virtue
Modesty
Dignity
And
Such trust

On this day
And
Always

You will know
What to do

Your precious soul
Will say
Look Maman
And
Remember

That I am here
With you
One day
This day
Always.

For Kirsten Elise Gabriel

SON

Vayu
Son
Of
The Wind

Apollo
Son
Of
The Sun

Oceanus
Oceanstream
Father
Of
Everything

Great Tree
Of
Life
Seed

As
Both
Father
And
Son
Of
This
Earth

You
Our
Son
Of
Wind

Flame
Sea
Firmament

Of
Courage
Blessing
Strength
Resilience
Nobility
Fortitude
Elegance
Kindness
Mercy

Of
Healing
Aspiring
Ascribing
Balance

Rooted
Trunk
Bark
Branches
Leaves
Buds
Into
Becoming

Fruit
Of
Wisdom
Benevolence
Gravity
And
Grace
Sap
Arising

Into
A
Canopy
Of
Forest

Son

For John Taylor Gabriel
At his Graduation from Medical School

ROSES

This
Late
Afternoon
When
Beneath
The
Indian Wells
Sun
Desert beauty
She was
As
The last
Rose petal
Fell
From
Her body
Her breath
Going
To God
Now
Gone
To Heaven
I should say
Full blown
Bower
Of blossoms
Of a good life
Perfumed
Grace
Showering
Humanity
With her
Hopes
Of goodness
Of that

Which
Might be
Three sons
May they
Bloom
In God
Everywhere
And
Always
For her
Their Mother's bouquet.

For Gail Walmsley Glass

SHE

She
Is

As
A
Fairy
Goddess
Heroine
Of
Some
Heavenly
Tale
Here
Now
On
Earth

Set
In
Clouds
Snowflakes
Mist
Of
Ocean
Breeze
Desert
Mountain
In
Sun
Star shine
Night sky
Alit
With
Fireflies
The Pleiades

Orion
And
The Milky Way

All
Prayer
Practice
Life
Divine

As
Upon
The
Flowering
Fields
Of
The Lord

She
Rides

A
Horse
Winged
By
Angel
Wings

Treading
The
Path
Of
Saints
Sages
Her
Father
Mother

Brothers
And their
Families
Ancestors
Mother Mary
And
Of
Grace

Humbly
Earnestly
Honorably
Beautifully

Prancing
Trotting
Cantering
Now
Galloping

She
Turns

As
Dervishes
Pray
For
Her
Husband
Hoped
Child
One
Or
More
God willing
Always

In
Her
Unveiled
Gaze
Luminous
Is
The flame
Of
That Great One's
Merciful
Candlelight

Her
Soul
Aligned
Ever
As
It
Should
Be
Each
Moment
Into
Eternity

She
Is

Blessed.

For Carolyn Grace Helminski Chadwick

VOICE

I.
Your
Arms

Which

Did
Not

Know
How

To
Hold

Me
Then

Father
Of
Mine

From
Heaven

Hold
Me
Now

II.
Your
Voice

Which

Sought
Freedom

Some
Mysterious

Place

Of
Meaning

Being
Self

Life
Love

Died

In
You

Wild
Man

My

Wild
Father

Of
Angst

Quest
Not

Fully
Known

III.
Your
Voice

I
Have

Always
Known

From
Before

I
Was

Born
As

You
Held

My
Mother

From
Before

I
Came

After
One

Sibling
Sister

And
Before

Two
Others

Brother
And
Sister

IV.
Your
Voice

Lullabying
Us

Inspiring
Teaching

Disappointing

Leaving
Us

V.
So
Angry

Was
I

At
Your

Voice
Your

Unawakened
Voice

My
Own

Young
Voice

Could
Not

Yet
Speak

Would
Not

Answer
You

My
Voice

Was
No

VI.
I
Needed

A
Shepherd

Good
Stoic

As
The

Moon
Sun

Stars
Mountains

How
Could

You
Not

Know

And

We
And

Mom
And

Family
But

Me
Dad

My
Voice

VII.
Because

I am

Your
Wild

Serene
Daughter

The
One

Free
Beyond
Angst

And

Sacred
In
Quest

Awakening

What
You

Could
Not
Yet

VIII.
Because
Somehow

In the
Perfection
Imperfection

Promise
Kept

Promise
Broken

Suffering
Loss

Faithless
Chaos

Regret
And
Death

Between
Our
Voices

Which
Could

Not
Then

Yet
Meet

IX.
In
Me

Blossoms
A ranch

A mountain wildflower
A great tree

A desert shrub
A garden

A family
A city

A civilization
A doctor

A woman
Daughter

X.
And

I
Hear

What
You
Could

Not
Say

As I
Did

Not
Come

To
You

On
The telephone

That
Day

As I
Listened

For you

My
Father

Your
Voice

Your
Real

Voice
Which

I
Would

Know
Anywhere

In
Eternity

To come
Home

XI.
To me
To Mom

To us all
To yourself
To God

XII.
Now
I know

For

My
Voice

Is
True

Your
Wild

Mustang
Daughter

Free
Noble

Faithful
So sensitive

On
The
Path

XIII.
Hold
Out

Your arms
Father
For me.

For Jacare Lauren Cardoza

HIS LOVE

My Brother has found a love
A great love
True and real
She is lovely
As trusted as the Birch stands of the far North
As deep as snowdrifts off the mountains
Of the high ranges
Or the Summer sky
Or the clear deep
Of the lakes
They so love

Innocent because she is good
She has chosen to live her life
As if it were a prayer
Or a jar of the finest honey
Cared for from bee to bud to flower to hive
To comb to pot to jar to sweeten
His soul, his heart, his body
And his life
My Brother
Has found his love.

A love has found my Brother
A great love
True and real
He is faithful
As aspiring as the Aurora of the far North
As devoted as the shepherds
Of all our World's continents
Wise because he is inspired to protect
Her soul, her heart, her body

He has chosen to live their lives
In gratitude
Fulfillment
And grace
For the sake of all
That he is
That she is
That they are
That they are
Blessed.

For Peter William Hin
and Beth Marie Putnam

THE LOVE OF MY LIFE

You are the love of my life
When I say this
I mean
You are the love of all of my lives
In Him who is
I find only
That
In you
In all ways
Always.

SANCTUARY

They stand

In
Her
Garden
As
If
They
Were
Married

He
Tall
And
Regarding
The
Wind
She
With
Eyes
As
If
A doe
And
Cutting Roses
Weaving Lavender

He mows
A
Vast swath
Of grasses
Beneath
The sun
And
Clouds
Discussing
The philosophy
Of
All
That
Is
With
His
Dogs
The sky
And

All

He moves
In a
Great
Old truck
Meadow
Ward
And
Toward
A
Forest
His
Forest
Glen

She gathers
A bouquet
Of the
Chores
And
Flowers
Of
This day
Every
Day

Sometimes
They
Bicker
Like
Crows
Over
Firewood
And
City plans
They
Fly
Away
He
Just
East
To
The pond
She
Just
West
To
The cutting beds
Of her herbs
To
Her table
Of craftwork
To the
Teacup
Of her friend
Or such

And he
Roosting
Once again
Day's end
Sun setting
Evening born
At
Their kitchen
Hearth
Crows
Is there
Enough
For me

She
Chirrups
Back
As
The
Songbird
Of
God
Hermit Thrush
Finch
Chickadee
Lark
Sparrow
Swallow
Which
She
Truly
Resembles
Enough

What
Dinner
Fruit
Wine
Clean clothes
Humor
Strong countenance
Energy of life
Challenge
Of
All
That is false
To truth
Just as
In
My heart

He
Answers
Responds
As a
Heron
Nighthawk
Peregrine
Owl
Eagle
Kingfisher
All
Birds
Children
Of God
Too

No dear
Enough love
Please

She
Deer~eyed
Wren~hearted
Sings
To him
Answers
In
Prayer
Faith
Knowledge
Wisdom
History
And
Grace
Always
My
Old crow
Impossible one
Young champion
Great protector
Fine man
My love

Always

They dine
Amidst
Hearts
Of
All
Forest
Creatures
Precious
Music
Of
All
Birds
In
Their
Shared
Soul
As if they were married

Bells ring in his temple
Beneath contented trees
Across the fields
Of their
Treasured
Holy home
And the flowers of
His wife's precious
Garden bloom
As if they were married.

For Joseph Kiefer and
Amy Goodman Kiefer

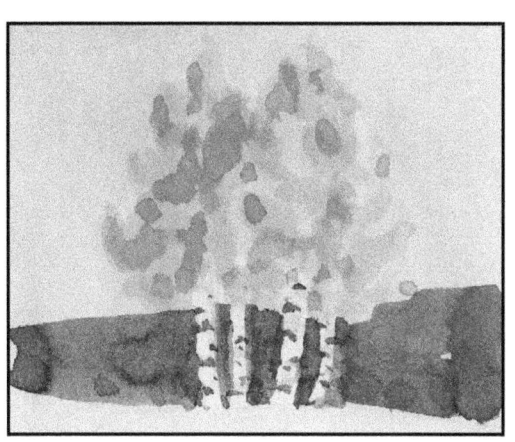

ABOUT THE AUTHOR

Elizabeth Anne Hin studied poetry formally with George E. Dimock, Richard Wilbur, William Hoover Van Voris, Michael Benedikt, Elizabeth Hardwick, Sir Stephen Spender, and Joseph Brodsky. Her Mother read poetry aloud from *A Child's Garden of Verses* by Robert Louis Stevenson and from other cherished texts from Beth's conception through childhood. Her Father taught her through his admiration for Homer's life, work, and virtuous message, from the world's classics and histories, and from noble and heroic peoples and cultures of all nations. He practiced his faith in the equality of all men and women, and in all aspiration: 'Ad astra per aspera,' ~Seneca. Her Mother was a private living example of this virtue.

Beth has embraced poetry, from reading to writing, since youth, observing in gratitude the poetry infused in sculpture at Wellington's port in New Zealand and attending readings by Jorge Luis Borges at the 92nd Street YMCA in Manhattan, New York, Adrienne Rich in a hallowed hall of Amherst, Massachusetts, Drummond Hadley and Gary Snyder in Anchorage, Alaska, Mary Oliver at a Presbyterian Church in Dallas, Texas. She has been shown kindness in mentoring by writers from John Updike to Carlos Fuentes, Richard Erdoes to Derek Walcott; and by W. S. Merwin, who expressed to her in 1973 that he had written nearly every day since the age of 21, and requested of Beth that she do the same.

ALSO BY ELIZABETH ANNE HIN

The Grail: A Story of Issa and Yeshua, 2014
Jdg: Poems of Love, 2016
Live Oak: Poems of Texas, 2016
Willow: Poems of Devotion, 2016
Sequoia: Poems of Eternity, 2018
Thistle: Poems of Life, 2018

Published by Issa Press, Austin Texas

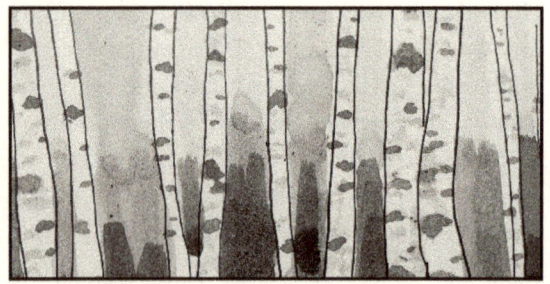

www.ingramcontent.com/pod-product-compliance
Lightning Source LLC
Chambersburg PA
CBHW022117090426
42743CB00008B/887